Discernment
for the
Ages

A Sermon on Wisdom in Turbulent Times

A 21st-Century Look at Proverbs 2:1-15

Richard Caldwell

Published by:
Kress Biblical Resources
www.kressbiblical.com

ISBN: 978-1-934952-60-3

Contents

Proverbs 2:1-15

My son, if you receive my words
  and treasure up my commandments with you,
[2] making your ear attentive to wisdom
  and inclining your heart to understanding;
[3] yes, if you call out for insight
  and raise your voice for understanding,
[4] if you seek it like silver
  and search for it as for hidden treasures,
[5] then you will understand the fear of the LORD
  and find the knowledge of God.
[6] For the LORD gives wisdom;
  from his mouth come knowledge and
understanding;
[7] he stores up sound wisdom for the upright;
  he is a shield to those who walk in integrity,
[8] guarding the paths of justice
  and watching over the way of his saints.
[9] Then you will understand righteousness and justice
  and equity, every good path;
[10] for wisdom will come into your heart,
  and knowledge will be pleasant to your soul;
[11] discretion will watch over you,
  understanding will guard you,
[12] delivering you from the way of evil,
  from men of perverted speech,
[13] who forsake the paths of uprightness
  to walk in the ways of darkness,
[14] who rejoice in doing evil
  and delight in the perverseness of evil,
[15] men whose paths are crooked,
  and who are devious in their ways.

INTRODUCTION...A WORLD IN CONFUSION

At the time of this writing, enormous things are happening in our world. Almost daily we meet with events that call for our attention, raise important questions, and prompt enormous conversation. As much as we sometimes wish that we could avoid what seems like constant turmoil, we cannot.

In recent months, we have been dealing with a virus that, at worst, was supposed to wipe out close to 2 million American citizens unless we took drastic measures. We were told that in the best-case scenario, hundreds of thousands of people would die if we did not take unprecedented steps of social isolation. We were told that we must all stay indoors and practice social distancing, or else we didn't love our neighbor. Circumstances, related to the crisis, were sometimes strange. There was a weird rush to buy toilet paper that we are still trying to understand. Hand sanitizer became more valuable than gold. All of this was unsettling, to say the least.

There were varying reports about how the virus was transmitted and what precautions were necessary to prevent infection. Maybe the virus was airborne, or maybe not. Perhaps masks are helpful, perhaps they are not. But due to the uncertainty of it all, there would be no exceptions made for these initial restrictions (regarding distancing), not a hospital visit, not a funeral service, not anything.

The result was that some people died completely separated from their families because hospitals would not allow visitors.

What seemed strange and confusing was that in the midst of all that danger there were "essential places" where infection could be risked. We could still congregate at general purpose stores like Walmart and Target. In some states, liquor stores were on the early list of "essential places." And as we've recently seen, apparently the virus is not to be feared at protests. There, we can stand shoulder to shoulder, sing and dance, and hang out for a few days. In fact, some of the very same health experts who staunchly insisted that there be no exceptions with respect to distancing guidelines that prohibited public gatherings, publicly threw their support behind various protests, or marches designed to make a social statement (such as a "gay pride" parade).

For the church, the major question about all this was not whether we would comply with the directives given by our governing officials. The Bible is clear in Romans 13 that we, as the church, are a submissive people. We are citizens of heaven, but we are also good citizens on earth. God calls us to submit to governing authorities. If we are not being asked to violate Scripture, then we are the most submissive and supportive of citizens. **The question all along has been, "How would the church think about this? How would the church process what was going on in the world around us?"**

And then, when we thought it couldn't get any more chaotic, just as it seemed we were beginning to emerge from the worst of the virus, we met with the tragic death of George Floyd.[1] The result of George Floyd's death has been a national conversation—indeed, it seems to be a global conversation— about race, about American history, and about the present condition of our society. At virtually every

---

[1] George Floyd was an African American who died, on camera, while in police custody.

turn, there are conversations about racism, about privilege, about how society is to be structured. **Once again, the major issue facing the church is, how do we think about these things? How do we see them? How do we process it?**

None of this is entirely new. It's just the latest in a world full of chaos and opinions. The world has always been full of opinions, but, because of social media, never have those opinions been so easily and broadly disseminated.

We've seen seismic shifts in culture during our lifetime. We have lived through the redefinition of marriage, something that to my knowledge was unprecedented in the history of the world. We are now living in a world that has embraced homosexuality, not as just something that should be tolerated, but as something good. In fact, if you pay attention to the television, you might think it is actually preferable. We have seen restroom facilities rearranged to accommodate people who insist that their gender is something separate from their biological sexual reality.

And through all these shifts and changes in culture, there has been an avalanche of activity intended— designed— to convince us that all of this is perfectly acceptable and normal. Virtually every major sports league, the entertainment industry, and the news media, have staked their place on the side of a new day in history when all these things are redefined. If you walk around average America, it's not so settled. But if you listen to what's coming through the airwaves of radio and television, it's seems as if this is settled. The ship has sailed. All that's left is for all of us to get on board.

The reeducation campaign isn't confined to adults. There are unmistakable attempts to influence the youngest among us. Whether it is what is taught in public school health classes, or the example set in some bizarre book reading given to children by men dressed like women, children are being indoctrinated.

What has been appalling and indicting through all of this, is how often the church has been found trying to avoid social disapproval. It is quite obvious, if we are paying attention, that the church is often found trying to "Christianize" whatever is trending in the current cultural consensus. All the while, of course, insisting that we are standing where we've always stood, holding on to our historic identity. We insist we're not compromising, but still it is apparent, we're trying to squeeze ourselves into a set of clothes we were never intended to wear. To use the biblical analogy of putting off and putting on (putting off the old dress that belonged to the old life and putting on the new dress that belongs to Christ), we are found trying to squeeze our way into the world's clothing, and yet claiming it's our own Christian brand.

How often the evangelical church of our time, has been willing to reevaluate what she has long believed, because of the social consciousness, the moral outrage, of a world that has already demonstrated that it has no conscience, and has no respect for what is truly moral according to Scripture! The church is often found speaking the same language, using the same jargon, and spouting the same perspectives, as a world in darkness.

Stop and think about it: Are we to believe that a world lost in sin, immersed in spiritual darkness, alienated from the life of God, so demonstrably wrong on so many issues, is suddenly supposed to be our guide concerning

- **How to live in this world?**

- **How to view race?**

- **How to view justice?**

Does the church suddenly need to take its cue from this world?

If the church were to choose a counselor, we couldn't choose a worse one. If the world becomes our counselor on these issues, understand that we have chosen a counselor that is the most unknowledgeable and unreasonable. It's a counselor that has a 100% track record of failure and has no fear of God. It is hopelessly selfish, a counselor who is blind, deaf, enslaved, and dead in sins, a counselor who is not a friend of the church. It is, in fact, a counselor whose doctrine has come from Satan.

When the church strives to be applauded by its world, it seeks the approval of a friend that only feigns loyalty. The world has never been the friend of the church — not the true church.

When the church strives to be the world's friend, it becomes the enemy of God. I'm not talking about a friend in the sense of redemption or in the sense of seeing people converted and transformed and loving Christ. Of course, the church is a friend to the world in that sense. We care about our world. We care about the lives of the people we meet with each day. But in terms of agreeing with the world's sense of morality and conscience, that represents enmity with God.

James 4:4 says: *You adulterous people! Do you not know that friendship with the world is enmity with God?*

Therefore whoever wishes to be a friend of the world makes himself an enemy of God.

These are straightforward and settled biblical truths. And yet, despite the reality of everything I've just said (about the world's counsel and approval), what do we see? Every step of the way, in all this confusion, there are loud voices that lecture us and warn us and shame us in the name of Christ. "Don't you love? Don't you care?" **And, according those voices, caring and loving are equated with a willingness to embrace evangelicalism's new version of the cultural narrative.** The culture says, "Here's how we're to think," and evangelicalism twists and contorts itself to fit in with the world's latest ideological fashions, all the while shaming anyone unwilling to do the same.

That's what is happening, and I warn you, it won't be the end of it. It's not the beginning of it, and it won't be the end of it, which is why I've entitled this book *Discernment for the Ages,* not "Discernment for the Moment," though what's here will certainly serve us in the moment. What I want us to see in the Word of God is for all times. It was good and trustworthy for the time in which it was written, it is true and sound this year, and it will be good and trustworthy for the rest of time, because it is the Word of God. It is not man's wisdom, but God's wisdom, which is what we need for every day, for every age, for every culture, for every time.

The church has a desperate need for discernment right now. If you pay any attention to social media, you'll see confusion, even among God's people. All kinds of arguments are taking place. Believers have always needed discernment and they always will. So, what does this

10

passage teach us about discernment? How is a believer to think? Whether we're dealing with a virus, or with racial conflict in society, how do we think about these things?

Reflection and Application

1. What are some of the major challenges that the world has faced lately?

2. What are some indications that the world's confused?

3. Should the church usually be quick to submit to government, or slow to submit? Why?

4. When should the church refuse to submit?

5. What are some major shifts in culture that you've lived through?

6. Should the evangelical church take its cues from the world's conscience?

7. How do you, personally, decide what's right and what's wrong?

THE DESIRE FOR DISCERNMENT

We'll be studying the first 15 verses of this second chapter in Proverbs. <u>The first point is found in verses 1-5, the desire for discernment.</u>

¹ My son, if you receive my words
* and treasure up my commandments with you,*
² making your ear attentive to wisdom
* and inclining your heart to understanding;*
³ yes, if you call out for insight
* and raise your voice for understanding,*
⁴ if you seek it like silver
* and search for it as for hidden treasures,*
*⁵ then you will understand the fear of the L*ORD
* and find the knowledge of God.*

The first thing we see in these verses, 1-15, is <u>the expression of desire.</u> And in addition, you find <u>a promise associated with that desire.</u> The pattern is: *If ..., if ..., if ..., then,* verse 5, *you will understand the fear of the L*ORD *and find the knowledge of God.*

Before we look at what the writer says here, I want to explain why I've chosen to use the word "discernment" to summarize what he's teaching us in verses 1-15. Even though you don't find the word "discernment" there, I believe "discernment" is a good word to summarize the whole passage. Discernment is what's called for, and discernment is what we should desire.

Why do I say that? Well, let me define it for a moment. **Discernment is the ability to set your approval on what God approves of, and to reject what God disapproves of, because you can tell the difference.** In the midst of all we're facing right now as a culture, are you able to recognize the difference between what God approves of and what He disapproves of, and are you setting your approval on what God approves of?

Discernment is <u>wisdom</u>. Discernment is <u>knowledge</u>. Discernment is <u>understanding</u>. Discernment is <u>discretion</u>, which gets to the matter of wise practice, **wisdom in practice**. If you and I really approve of what God approves of, <u>it will be more than an attitude</u>. It's going to penetrate to the depths of what we see, how we perceive life, and what our perspective is. That then influences our attitudes, our words, and our choices.

Hebrews 5:4 *But solid food is for the mature, for those who have their powers of discernment trained by constant practice to distinguish good from evil.*

Or, as the New American Standard Bible puts it, *who because of practice have their senses trained to discern good and evil.* This involves practice, a habit. It involves exercising or training our senses, our organs of perception—what we see, what we hear. It involves training them to discern, to pass judgment, on what's good and what's evil.

<u>That's what discernment is. You're able to distinguish good from evil</u>. And the reason you're able to distinguish good from evil is that you have been practicing discretion by using the Word of God. Your spiritual organ of perception has been trained by the truth of God. It's a process. It takes time. It means walking with God, knowing the Word of God, and practicing Scripture. The more you do this, day after day, month after month, year after year, the more you grow in your ability to distinguish good from evil. distinguishing between what God actually approves of,

and what He disapproves of, so that you focus your mind, heart, will, and desires on what is pleasing to God.

And the standard for discernment is the Word of God. It is the teaching of God's wisdom that produces wisdom if you receive it properly. Where do you get wisdom? You get it from the Word of God.

With the word "discernment" in mind, next we'll notice some of the elements that are identified here for us to have discernment. We have to desire it. We have to truly want it. And the first element of that involves the teaching of wisdom.

Reflection and Application

1. Re-read the definition of discernment. Explain each part of it.

2. What are some other words that can be used in place of the word "discernment"?

3. Why is discernment more than an attitude?

4. What does practice have to do with discernment?

5. What does maturity have to do with wisdom?

6. What is the standard for discernment?

7. In what ways has the Bible changed your own beliefs about what's good and what's bad?

THIS IS A CONCERN FOR ALL WHO LOVE (vs. 1)

<u>The desire for discernment shows itself in the person who loves other people</u>. This instruction is given to us in the language of a father teaching a son. Verse 1: *My son,*—this is a father teaching a son, or you could use the same sort of language to talk about a discipler teaching a student. There is often that kind of father/son relationship between someone who is discipling and someone who is learning.

But the point is, <u>if you really love another person, you want them to have discernment</u>. You want them to be able to distinguish between what is good and what is evil, what is right and what is wrong, what is pleasing to God and what isn't. So that, in these verses, you have a father pleading with his son to receive the words, the commandments that will result in wisdom. *My son, if you receive my words and treasure up my commandments with you, making your ear attentive to wisdom and inclining your heart to understanding....* In other words, I want to give you wisdom. I want to give you the words of God. And my desire for you is that you'll heed them; that you'll, hear them, and receive them. If you really love another person, discernment matters.

Parents, do you care that your children would have an accurate view of the world and its issues? Particularly at this point in time, if you've not been alerted to the need for you to take your children diligently to the Word of God and teach them how to think through life, you are failing in a major responsibility as a parent. This is <u>your job</u>. But for you to be good teachers, you have to be good learners. The <u>church's job</u> is to teach you the Word of God in such a way that you are then equipped to teach your family so that your children will emerge from your home one day, wise. You can't love someone and be indifferent to the subject of discernment.

Pastors, do you care that the church you shepherd walks with God? In the midst of a world of confusion do want to see your congregation stabilized in truth, not tossed to and fro with every wind of doctrine and every cultural whim, but able to walk with stability in the Word of God? Does it matter? Is that what you want? Do you want the people you love to walk with God in the safety of God's truth because that's the only safe ground there is? Do you want to see lives produced that are a force for good, for true justice, for righteousness, for godliness, and for every good way forward?

Do you care that the people you love would have the necessary equipment to live like this even when you're not around? When the day comes that you're not there anymore, do you want to have taught them in such a way that they have wisdom, discretion, and discernment without you, pointing them every step of the way to God and to His Word, so that they're equipped to be able to recognize the differences?

Reflection and Application

1. Why should you want the people you love to have discernment?

2. What is a parent's job concerning a child's growth in discernment?

3. What is a pastor's job concerning a congregation's growth in discernment?

4. What does your future absence have to do with their discernment?

5. Name a few people whom you love. How are you striving to improve their ability to discern the difference between what pleases God and what displeases Him?

THIS IS A CONCERN FOR ALL WHO HEED THAT LOVE (vss. 1-5)

So, the first desire you see in the first five verses is that of the teacher. He has his son in his heart. He has wisdom in his mouth, and he wants his son to receive these sayings. But notice that he's also giving voice to a concern that ought to exist in the people being loved. <u>It ought not just to be the person who loves who cares about discernment, but the people being loved must also care about discernment.</u>

The father is calling upon his son to care about what he cares about. "I am pleading with you to receive the words of God, the commandments that are in my mouth for you. I'm pleading with you to receive these things because I want you to have wisdom," which means that if the son heeds the voice of his father, he will care to receive what his father is teaching. Like his father, he will care about discernment.

<u>You can't love and respect someone who is wiser than you, and loves you, if you don't care about discernment.</u> It's true in a home as well as in a church. It's true among any two people that love each other. If a person who is wiser in the Lord and more knowledgeable in the Word of God than you are, and they are seeking to teach you something for the sake of the pleasantness of your soul and for the safety of your life, as the writer says here, if <u>they care</u> enough to teach you truth, then <u>you must care</u> enough to hear it, to receive it.

Every wise teacher knows that there is only one place where all wisdom resides—in Christ. None of us can claim that we have all wisdom, because we do not. Every wise teacher knows that. But listen: <u>every wise learner still holds wise teachers in high regard. Every wise learner says, "I need to listen to my teachers."</u> That's especially true where

God has assigned teaching responsibility. Pastors are responsible to shepherd the church. The church should acknowledge and respect that. Parents are responsible to shepherd their children. Children should understand and respect that. That's wisdom.

Currently, we are suffering from a self-willed culture, from a kind of independence that is very unwise. <u>Social media has certainly underscored in people the wrong instinct that I have a voice, and my voice must be heard.</u> And so, here I am sort of speaking just for me. It is the kind of pride that imagines that the world has just begun: <u>Every man doing what's right in his own eyes, saying what's right according to his own mind</u> (think about the period of the judges in the Bible). **And we have forgotten that the church is the pillar and support of the truth in the world.**

Has anyone stopped to ask, "What does our church believe about this? Where does our church stand on this? What do our elders say about this?" Before I go spouting off my ideas, maybe I should stop and ask, "What do my teachers say?" Am I willing to listen? Before children are spouting off their ideas, have they stopped to ask, "What do my parents say about this? Are they giving me the Word of God?"

We are suffering because of an age that has taught HIGH SELF-CONFIDENCE in people who have LOW COMPETENCE. For the last 20 to 30 years (maybe longer), our country has taught young people, "You're the greatest. You're the best. There's nothing you can't do." So, you have these people walking around with high confidence in themselves, but low competence when it comes to the way they think. Low competence is bad enough, but when low competence is joined to high confidence, you have a force for destruction. And that is all over our culture. You have people absolutely convinced they know what's best when they don't have a clue about what's best.

One of the marks of foolishness is apathy about these God-given assignments, these God-given relationships (pastor/church, parent/child). There's a willingness to tear down those relationships that God has chosen for the advancement of wisdom. We are suffering from a lack of biblical ecclesiology (the study of God's design for the church: what it is, who's in it, and how it functions). As I said earlier, every man does what is right in his own eyes— just giving voice to his own thoughts, and no one asks, "What does the church say?"

Reflection and Application

1. How does caring about discernment show love and respect for someone who is wiser than you, and who loves you?

2. Why is it wise to listen to your teachers?

3. Why is it a good idea not to share all of your thoughts on social media?

4. Have you considered asking your church leaders for wisdom concerning your ideas?

5. Why is high confidence often a bad thing?

6. Explain why apathy concerning God-given relationships is foolish.

7. Read Judges 21:25 in the Bible and ponder it.

REQUIREMENTS FOR DISCERNMENT (vss. 1-5)

We not only see the desire for discernment in these verses, but we see that there are requirements if one is to learn this kind of wisdom. It's not enough to say, "I desire to be discerning." If you desire the ability to recognize what pleases God and what doesn't, are you willing then to embrace the requirements for that?

You'll find a series of *IF* statements, and then there's a series of *THEN* statements. *If* this is true.... *Then* this will be the result. So, the *IF*s represent a series of requirements for discernment. You may want to make a visual chart of all of the *IF* statements and all of the *THEN* statements in these verses. "*...if you receive my words,*" "*if you call out for insight,*" "*if you seek it like silver,*" "*then,*" "*then,*" "*then....*" If you want the *THEN*, you have to embrace the *IF*s. Keeping that in mind, you could ask: What is required if I'm to have a discerning life?

A receptive heart—we are willing to receive (vss. 1-2)

The first thing you see is that you must have a receptive heart. *My son, if you receive my words and treasure up my commandments with you, making your ear attentive to wisdom and inclining your heart to understanding; yes, if you call out for insight...* and on he goes.

What becomes clear is that a receptive heart is more than just a willingness to listen passively. It's not, "Okay, I'll hear you out." It is listening with attentiveness. He says in verse 2 that you must *receive* his words, *making your ear attentive to wisdom*. You must be *inclining your heart*—the picture of bowing almost—to understanding. He's calling for a kind of listening that is attentive, accepting, and submissive to the teaching. If you really have a receptive heart, your purpose in listening is to learn and to obey. If you want discernment, then you have to be an obedient listener to the Word of God.

A perceptive heart—we see the value of what we receive (vss.1b-5)

Second, we need not only a receptive heart, but a perceptive heart. This son not only would be willing to listen, but he understands the goodness and value of what he's receiving, because we see in verse 2 that he is called to treasure up these commandments within him.

Holding on to what we are given (vs. 1b).
You perceive its value.

Treasure them up because you realize they're treasure. Hold on to what you've been taught, he's saying. To treasure them up is to store them away, hide them away, put away for safe keeping. You want to protect it, guard it, and cherish it, because you recognize its value and don't want to lose it. Take what you've been taught from the Word of God and hide it away within your heart. Keep it safe there, because it's valuable.

Yielding to what we are given (vs. 2b).
You perceive its authority.

You have a heart that perceives the value of the teaching, of wisdom, so that you yield to what you're given. **You perceive not only its value; you perceive its authority**. "Why? Why would I make my ear attentive to it? Why would I incline my heart to it?" Because you realize that what your father is giving you, in this case in Proverbs 2, is not just his opinion. These are the words of God. They have authority, so you want to yield yourself to what you're being taught.

I can say it to you this way: a heart that perceives the true nature of Scripture will be subject to its authority.

You recognize its source and its nature. In your Bible you have something that has come to us from God.

You recognize its truthfulness. Because it's come to us from God, it is altogether truthful. As a whole, it is truth. In every one of its statements, it is true. So, if you want the truth in the midst of a confusing world, where are you going to find it? In the Word of God.

You recognize its authority. You come to the Scripture in order to obey it, not to test it.

You recognize its sufficiency. In it, God gave us everything we need for life and godliness. Because you realize all of this, you listen to it differently.

You hear it in a singular way. It's not one voice in the midst of a world full of voices. It is the only voice that matters in a world full of voices. You hear the Word of God that way.

Seeking for what we need (vs. 3-4).
You pursue it.

The heart that perceives the authority of the words of God will seek after them, pursue them.

Verse 3: *yes, if you call out for insight...* Now you're not just passively listening. You're seeking. *...if you call out for insight and raise your voice for understanding, if you seek it like silver and search for it as for hidden treasures....*

If I told you there's a million dollars' worth of gold buried somewhere in your house, how would you seek it? And he says, "You know what? You must seek for wisdom the way you would seek for silver, or the way you would seek for hidden treasure." You're seeking, pursuing wisdom because you know that you need it.

Proverbs 8:17 (Wisdom is personified here.) *I love those who love me, and those who seek me diligently find me.*

Proverbs 16:16 *How much better to get wisdom than gold! To get understanding is to be chosen rather than silver.*

Proverbs 8:10 (Again, wisdom is personified.) *Take my instruction instead of silver, and knowledge rather than choice gold...."*

Compare the amount of effort people spend trying to make money with the amount even those in the church spend in trying to get the wisdom of God, especially given the fact that we're given promises about this.

James 1:5 *If any of you lacks wisdom, let him ask God, who gives generously to all without reproach, and it will be given him.*

In the face of such statements, I am amazed at professing Christians who are content to simply repeat what they're hearing from the world around them! I'm amazed at how little thought has gone into what professing believers have accepted as true and right simply because they are immersed in it. When the church finds itself parroting what the world says about any issue, it is repeating ideas, perspectives, and philosophies that at the very least, we can say are lying on the surface of the ground where just anybody can take hold of them. If the world can grasp it, then it is knowledge you can get without God, without conversion and without the Spirit of God.

But what you and I are called to seek for is something that <u>doesn't lie on the surface of the ground</u>. It has to be sought, pursued. You have to desire it more than you desire anything in this world. That's when you'll find it. It's something you have to seek for diligently. It's not natural to people. It represents revelation from heaven—something supernatural that has come from the throne of God. It's not just lying on the surface of the ground, and those without Christ certainly don't have access to it. That's what you need right now in the midst of all this confusion. You don't need what lies on the surface that just anybody can grab hold of. You need what comes from heaven. I tell you, it will not <u>sound</u> the same as what the world is saying and it will not <u>be</u> the same as what the world is saying.

A humble heart—looking to God for these things—we strive to understand the fear of the Lord (vss. 3-5a)

What is required for discernment? You need have to have a <u>receptive</u> and <u>perceptive heart.</u> And if you do, you'll understand <u>the value of God's words</u>, the <u>authority of God's Word</u>, and <u>your need for God's Word</u>. So that we can also say this is the <u>humble heart</u>. Where does wisdom reside? In the humble heart. This is the heart that seeks for God.

In verse 5 we find our *THEN* statement after all the *IF*s: *then you will understand the fear of the LORD and find the knowledge of God.* This is what we're after, not the wisdom of men, but the fear of the Lord, the knowledge of God. And by the way, the whole Bible is sometimes described in this way. Psalm 19 describes the Word of God as the fear of the

Lord. Notice how *the fear of the Lord* is parallel to various descriptions of God's Word:

Psalm 19:7–11 *The law of the LORD is perfect,*
reviving the soul;
the testimony of the LORD is sure,
making wise the simple;
⁸ the precepts of the LORD are right,
rejoicing the heart;
the commandment of the LORD is pure,
enlightening the eyes;
⁹ the fear of the LORD is clean,
enduring forever;
the rules of the LORD are true,
and righteous altogether.
¹⁰ More to be desired are they than gold,
even much fine gold;
sweeter also than honey
and drippings of the honeycomb.
¹¹ Moreover, by them is your servant warned;
in keeping them there is great reward.

Humility is why you're willing to listen, and why you do submit, and why you're seeking. Your heart is humble, not lifted up with the pride of low competence and high confidence. Rather, you understand what you don't have.

Pride won't listen and won't submit, because it already has what it needs. But if you want discernment there has to be the lowly heart that says, "I value the words of God. I need the words of God, and I won't be satisfied with anything but the words of God. I want God's wisdom."

A believing heart—the outcome has been announced (vs. 5)

This attitude means you'll have a believing heart, because verse 5 represents a promise, doesn't it? *Then you will understand the fear of the LORD....* When you seek like this, seeking where you should seek, and with the attitude you should seek with, God says you're going to find what you want. This distinguishes discernment from the wisdom of the age. <u>Discernment is found in the fear and the revelation of God.</u>

Let me tell you where discernment is not found. **It's not found in your emotions, and it's not found in your experiences.** We are living in a world right now that is emoting itself to death, full of emotion and error, and claiming a wisdom found in personal experience that is not wisdom. It's just experience—not transformed by the wisdom of God.

There is a doctrine that is gaining traction in our culture, that you are not qualified to know or to say anything about anything that doesn't involve your personal experience. Men can't say anything about women's issues because they're not women. People with light skin can't say anything about any issue that intersects with people who have dark skin because they don't have dark skin. "Just shut up and listen." That's the attitude.

What this doctrine assumes is that wisdom is found in one's feelings or in one's experiences. The Bible doesn't agree with that. **Wisdom is not found within you, not in your emotions, and not even in your experiences. Wisdom is found with God and in His Word.** In fact, some of the worst thinking you'll ever hear comes from people right in the midst of an experience. "Pastor, I know what the Bible says about marriage, but you haven't lived in my marriage." And out they come with all of their ideas about what ought to be right, because they're in the midst of a bad marriage. They think that if I were in the midst of a bad marriage, then I would have a better understanding.

No, listen. What you're saying in the midst of your bad marriage doesn't agree with Scripture, which means your experiences have done nothing except colored your perspective. And what is true in that one illustration is true with anything else you want to talk about. **Wisdom is not found in one's emotions or experiences. It is found in God's Word**. **You look away from yourself, if you're going to know the truth.** In fact, if we're telling anybody to shut up, we should tell ourselves to shut up. "Richard, just shut up and listen to God's Word," because that's where wisdom is found. **You have to realize that the truth is the truth, and it's determined by God and not by you, and not by popular vote**. It is not found by looking within people. It is found by looking <u>away</u> from yourself, <u>away</u> from your culture, and by looking <u>to</u> God and His Word. This is why we can seek for wisdom in faith.

Reflection and Application

1. Is your heart receptive to God's wise instruction in the Bible?

2. What is your perception as to the Scripture's nature? Where did it come from?

3. Do you hang on to what you're taught by Scripture and by wise, godly teachers?

4. Do you yield to Scripture's truthfulness and authority?

5. Do you believe Scripture is sufficient to tell us what we need to know about God and about the nature and purpose of mankind?

6. Do you listen to Scripture in a way that you don't listen to any other voices?

7. Do you pursue wisdom regularly and eagerly?

8. Would those who try to teach you describe you as humble or proud?

9. Which do you believe more—God's promises or your experience?

THE GIVER OF DISCERNMENT (vss. 6-8)

Understand that the entire culture could agree on what is right and be entirely wrong where it doesn't agree with Scripture. That brings us to the giver of discernment. You want it and are ready to receive it, but where do you go?

Verse 6: *For the LORD gives wisdom; from his mouth come knowledge and understanding; he stores up sound wisdom for the upright; he is a shield to those who walk in integrity, guarding the paths of justice and watching over the way of his saints.*

This verse repeatedly tells you where to go to find wisdom: *For the LORD gives wisdom; from his mouth come knowledge and understanding; he stores up sound wisdom for the upright; he is a shield to those who walk in integrity....* Where do you go for discernment? You go to God.

And the only people who will go to Him and receive this, the only people who go to the right source, are described in verse 7 where it says that *he stores up sound wisdom for the upright....* Who receives from the hand of God? People who, verse 7, *walk in integrity.* Whose ways will God watch over? Verse 8: *the way of his saints.* This isn't a worldly concept of uprightness, nor a worldly concept of integrity, but something that is altogether holy. The saints of God look to the words of God and go to the source of discernment. And there they will find discernment and wisdom. Who gives discernment? God gives discernment.

Reflection and Application

1. Where do most people look for wisdom and discernment?

2. What's wrong with their approach?

3. Where does Proverbs 2:6 say that wisdom comes from?

4. What sort of people are able to receive wisdom?

5. Are you that kind of person? If not, what will you do about it?

6. When was the last time you asked the Lord for discernment or wisdom?

THE FRUITS OF DISCERNMENT (vss. 9-15)

In verses 9-15, you find the <u>fruits of discernment</u>. There's another *THEN* statement. Once I have met the conditions, once the *IF*s are in place...

- when my attitude toward wisdom is what these verses describe
- when my actions regarding wisdom are as these verses describe
- when I see the source of wisdom as these verses describe
- when verses 1-8 become my life

THEN verses 9-15 will be the result—the fruits of discernment.

I could ask it this way: What will characterize your life if you reject the world's wisdom and you walk in God's wisdom? What will your life look like if you reject the world's narrative and you accept the Word of God? Something beautiful is described for us.

You will walk on safe ground. (vss. 8b-9)

What does God do? He guards. Verse 8, He guards *the paths of justice*. Do you want to know what justice is? It's what the Bible says it is. The Word of God is upright. The law of God is upright. It is just. Justice is what God says it is. Stop taking your concepts of justice from Marxism. Stop taking your concepts of justice from Republicanism and stop taking your concepts of justice from man's wisdom. Look to the Word of God.

God guards *the paths of justice* and watches over *the way of his saints*. What is safe ground? <u>Safe ground is the</u>

ground of God's wisdom—the ground of God's Word. Go to the Lord, and you'll to walk on safe ground. Go to the Lord, and you'll live your life with a sound mind.

You will walk with a sound mind (vss. 10-11)

What we're seeing right now in our culture is insanity on display. The way people are living at the moment defies even basic logic. But if you walk in the wisdom of God, you have soundness of mind and heart. Look at verse 10. When you do this, ...*wisdom will come into your heart, and knowledge will be pleasant to your soul....* You will love what's true and right, and it will be pleasing to you. It will be a blessing to your own soul. ...*discretion will watch over you, understanding will guard you*—don't miss that connection. God guards the paths of His children. How does He do it? He does it through the understanding and the knowledge He gives them.

Obviously, God guards us providentially through circumstances and in other ways, but He also guards us with truth. He teaches us the way in which to walk, and when we give heed to Him, when we live this life of wisdom, and listen to God, now we're walking on that safe ground. And in that way, God is guarding us, watching over us and protecting us. You'll live your life with a sound mind.

I pray for you. Pray for me. I pray that you'll be able to turn a deaf ear to the culture and open your ear wide to God and His Word. May the Lord help us.

You will not walk in the counsel of the wicked. (vss. 12-15)

You will reject their ways. (vs. 12a)

Verse 12 says, as God is watching over you and guarding you, etc., He will be delivering you from something—...*delivering you from the way of evil*.... If I am discerning, I can recognize what's good and what isn't. I'm going to walk in the pathway of God's Word, which is the good, which <u>means I'll be delivered from another kind of way, from a way that is evil.</u> Evil finds expression in this world in people. And so, I'm going to reject evil ways found in men.

You will reject their speech. (vs. 12b)

As verse 12 says, ...*delivering you from the way of evil, from men of perverted speech*.... I'm going to reject walking with evil people, which means <u>I'm going to reject their speech</u>. ...*from men of perverted speech*.... If anything ought to tip you off to the fact the world doesn't have the current issues right, just turn on YouTube and listen to the words they're using. Listen to all the perversion being spewed forth in the name of justice, in the name of what's right; it's full of perverted speech. God's people must not be yoked to such things.

You will reject their values (vs. 13)

<u>Not only do we reject their ways and their words.</u> We reject <u>their values</u>. Verse 13*: who forsake the paths of uprightness to walk in the ways of darkness*.... You can't walk in the way of darkness without rejecting what's light. This is what the world does at every turn. It rejects what is truly upright to pursue what is darkness. Many of the same people crying out right now for justice, wholeheartedly support the slaughter of millions of babies in the womb every year. The people that the church is seemingly afraid of not listening to, are the very same people who contend for acceptance of LGBTQ (add the initials).

Can you recognize that there is a way of evil, and there is a way of uprightness? <u>And those who walk in the wisdom of God must reject their ways, and therefore, reject their words, which means rejecting their values.</u> **What are our values?**

You will reject their delights. (vs. 14)

Look at verse 14: *who rejoice in doing evil and delight in the perverseness of evil*—they take pleasure in what God hates. They must not be the people we walk with.

You will reject their deviations. (vs. 15)

Verse 15: *men whose paths are crooked, and who are devious in their ways.* They pursue that which deviates from God's standard, a departure from what is right in the sight of God.

The longer the frog stays in the kettle, so to speak, the harder it becomes for a professing church that isn't saturated with Scripture to be able to recognize where the deviations are occurring. Perhaps they are well-meaning people, perhaps even some converted people, who are suffering because of their ignorance of truth, and what they're hearing all around them sounds so convincing, that they can't tell the difference.

What we've just seen in Proverbs 2:1-15 is embodied in the 1st Psalm. If you want to live a blessed life, then you'll want to read what this psalm says.

*[1] Blessed is the man
    who walks not in the counsel of the wicked,
nor stands in the way of sinners,
    nor sits in the seat of scoffers;*

² but his delight is in the law of the LORD,
  and on his law he meditates day and night.

³ He is like a tree
  planted by streams of water
that yields its fruit in its season,
  and its leaf does not wither.
In all that he does, he prospers.
⁴ The wicked are not so,
but are like chaff that the wind drives away.
⁵ Therefore the wicked will not stand in the judgment,
  nor sinners in the congregation of the righteous;
⁶ for the LORD knows the way of the righteous,
  but the way of the wicked will perish.

Reflection and Application

1. How does discernment relate to safety?

2. How does discernment relate to sound thinking?

3. How does wisdom protect you from evil ways?

4. Are you rejecting the ways, the speech, and the values of this world? Or do you generally act like the world, talk like the world, and evaluate like the world?

5. Do you ever take pleasure in things that the Lord hates? If so, are you willing to repent of that?

6. Do you endorse things that are perversions of the Lord's design?

7. Are you willing to seek wisdom and discernment as a treasure? If so, what blessings will result?

CONCLUSION

God's people will be distinguished by their relationship to God's Word. The reason why we are a people completely committed to His Word, is that we recognize that it is God's wisdom. What we want is not the wisdom of the age, but the wisdom of God. That is why we seek it, we hear it, and we bow our hearts to it. We submit our lives to it and walk in it, not just for today's issue, but for the issues that preceded it and for the issues that will follow it. We live in a world that will always be filled with chaos and opinions until Jesus comes. But we are a people who live our lives on the words of God.

And so, I exhort you, as the 1st verse of Proverbs 2 does, to **listen to words of wisdom**, which are the commands of God found in His Word. **Incline your heart there. Reject the world's narrative and know that God's wisdom will never sound like it and will never be like it. Go to the Word of God, listen to your teachers, and ask, "What is wisdom for this situation?"**

PRAYER

Our Father in heaven, thank You that we are not without truth. Your Word is the truth. Our Savior prayed for us that we would be sanctified in the truth, and then He said, "Your Word is truth." Your church, Lord, is to be the pillar and support of the truth in this world, not spouting the philosophies, the vain ideas of the wisdom of the age, but preaching and teaching Scripture carefully, submissively, humbly, knowing that truth is not found in our emotions or in our experiences, but is found in Your Word. Strengthen us, Lord, to live lives that really are countercultural, but not simply for that reason, but because as Romans 12 teaches us, Lord, we must resist being conformed to this world in order to be transformed by the renewal of our minds. Help us, Lord, to reject the culture's narrative so that we might receive Yours, and be transformed in the process into the image of our Savior, the perfect One, the Savior that You've given to the world, the One who can deliver sinners from our vain ideas and from our vain lives, and give us what is life indeed. Put us in our right mind as the writer of Proverbs says in chapter 2, that our hearts then would find wisdom within them that would be pleasantness to our souls. Lord, may You do this in my life and in the lives of readers of this little book. May You make much of Yourself in our small lives by filling us up with the truth as it is in Jesus. We ask for this in Jesus' name. Amen.

www.ingramcontent.com/pod-product-compliance
Lightning Source LLC
Chambersburg PA
CBHW071652040426
42452CB00009B/1848